Dictionary of

Biological Psychology

James W. Kalat
North Carolina State University

Brooks/Cole Publishing Company

I(T)P   An International Thomson Publishing Company

Pacific Grove • Albany • Bonn • Boston • Cincinnati • Detroit
London • Madrid • Melbourne • Mexico City • New York • Paris
San Francisco • Singapore • Tokyo • Toronto • Washington

Sponsoring Editor: Faith B. Stoddard
Editorial Assistant: Patsy Vienneau
Production Coordinator: Tessa A. McGlasson
Cover Design: Roy R. Neuhaus
Cover Illustration: Jeena Keller
Printing and Binding: Malloy Lithographing, Inc.

For more information, contact:

Brooks/Cole Publishing Company
511 Forest Lodge Road
Pacific Grove, CA 93950
USA

International Thomson Publishing—Europe
Berkshire House 168-173
High Holborn
London WC1V 7AA
England

International Thomson Publishing Gmbh
Königwinterer Strasse 418
53227 Bonn
Germany

Thomas Nelson Australia
102 Dodds Street
South Melbourne, 3205
Victoria, Australia

International Thomson Publishing—Asia
221 Henderson Road #05-10
Henderson Building
Singapore 0315

Nelson Canada
1120 Birchmount Road
Scarborough, Ontario
Canada M1K 5G4

International Thomson Publishing—Japan
Hirakawacho-cho Kyowa Building, 3F
2-2-1 Hirakawacho-cho
Chiyoda-ku, Tokyo 102
Japan

Printed in the United States of America.

5   4   3   2

ISBN 0-534-26010-1

Dictionary of Biological Psychology

Note on alphabetization: Terms that begin with a number, such as 6-hydroxydopamine and 5-hydroxytryptophan, are listed under the main part of the word (hydroxydopamine and hydroxytryptophan), as if there were no number. Greek symbols are alphabetized as if they were spelled out; for example, b- is listed as if it were beta-.)

a- prefix meaning lack of, absence of

abasia inability to walk

abducens nerve the sixth cranial nerve, carrying sensations from eye muscles and contolling eye movements

ablation removal of a structure

absence seizure type of generalized seizure in which the person stares, unresponsive to the environment, for a period of seconds, making no sudden movements, except perhaps for eyeblinking or a drooping of the head

absolute refractory period time immediately after an action potential, when the membrane cannot produce an action potential in response to stimulation of any intensity

accessory nerve the eleventh cranial nerve, controlling movements of shoulders and head, and parasympathetic nerves to the viscera

acetaldehyde toxic substance produced in the metabolism of alcohol

acetaldehyde dehydrogenase enzyme that converts acetaldehyde to acetic acid

acetic acid chemical that the body uses as a source of energy

acetylcholine chemical that acts as a neurotransmitter

acetylcholinesterase enzyme that breaks acetylcholine into acetate and choline

ACh acetylcholine

AChE acetylcholinesterase

across-fiber pattern theory notion that each receptor responds to a wide range of stimuli and contributes to the perception of every stimulus in its system

ACTH adrenocorticotropic hormone, which stimulates the adrenal cortex to release cortisol

action potential depolarization of an axon produced by a stimulation beyond the threshold

activating effect temporary effect of a hormone on behavior or anatomy, occurring only while the hormone is present

activation-synthesis hypothesis hypothesis that the brain synthesizes dreams from spontaneous brain activity occurring during sleep

active sleep synonym for REM sleep

active transport transfer of chemicals across a membrane by expenditure of energy as opposed to passive diffusion

acuity the ability to separate or resolve adjacent visual stimuli

acute having a sudden onset

adaptation decreased response to a stimulus as a result of recent exposure to it

ADD attention-deficit disorder

ADDH attention-deficit disorder with hyperactivity

adrenocorticotropic hormone hormone that stimulates the adrenal cortex to release cortisol

adenohypophysis the anterior pituitary

adenosine chemical that acts as a neurotransmitter

ADH antidiuretic hormone

adipsia lack of drinking

adrenalin synonym for epinephrine

AF64A drug that destroys synapses that use acetylcholine as their neurotransmitter

affective attack attack in which an animal shows signs of emotional arousal

affective psychosis or **affective illness** disorder characterized by mood disorders, such as depression or mania

afferent axon a neuron that brings information into a structure

affinity tendency of a drug to bind to a particular type of receptor

agenesis failure to develop

ageusia deficient sense of taste

agnosia inability to recognize or identify stimuli

agonist drug that mimics or increases the effects of a neurotransmitter

agraphesthesia the inability to recognize figures written on the skin

akinesia lack of movement

aldosterone adrenal hormone that causes the kidneys to conserve sodium when excreting urine

alexia inability to read

all-or-none law principle that the size and shape of the action potential are independent of the intensity of the stimulus that initiated it

alpha-fetoprotein protein found in the bloodstream of most immature mammals that binds with estrogen

alpha-methyl-para-tyrosine a chemical similar to tyrosine; it attaches to the enzyme that metabolizes tyrosine into dopa, thus preventing the enzyme from performing its usual task. The result is a decrease in the synthesis of dopa, and therefore also of dopamine, norepinephrine, and epinephrine.

alpha wave rhythm of 8 to 12 brain waves per second, generally associated with relaxation

altruism acting to help another individual without immediate or direct benefit to oneself

Alzheimer's disease condition characterized by memory loss, confusion, depression, restlessness, hallucinations, delusions, and disturbances of eating, sleeping, and other daily activities

amacrine cell local neuron within the eye having no axon

amblyopia ex anopsia reduced vision resulting from disuse of an eye, usually associated with failure of the two eyes to point in the same direction

amiloride drug that blocks the passage of sodium ions through a membrane

amino acid an acid containing an amine group (NH_2); one of the components of peptides

amnesia memory loss

amphetamine strong stimulant drug that increases the release of dopamine and blocks the reuptake of dopamine by the presynaptic neuron

amphetamine psychosis condition resembling schizophrenia provoked by a large dose of amphetamine

amplitude the intensity of a sound or other stimulus

AMPT see alpha-methyl-para-tyrosine

ampulla a dilation at one end of each semicircular canal of the vestibular system

amygdala brain area located within the temporal lobe of the cerebral cortex

amyloid *see* **b-amyloid**

amyotrophic lateral sclerosis (Lou Gehrig's disease) disease that produces gradual weakness and paralysis, due to loss of motor neurons in the spinal cord and loss of axons from the brain to the spinal cord

amytal drug that can be used either to tranquilize or to anesthetize the brain, depending on dose

analgesia relief from pain

anandamide a naturally-occurring brain chemical that stimulates the same receptors as cannabinoids

androgen a class of steroid hormones more abundant in males than in females for most species

androgen insensitivity condition in which a person lacks the mechanism that enables androgens to bind to genes in a cell's nucleus

anesthesia lack of sensation

anesthetic drug that blocks sensation

angiotensin II hormone that constricts the blood vessels

anisomycin drug that inhibits protein synthesis

anomia inability to remember the names of objects

anorexia loss of appetite

anorexia nervosa condition in which a person refuses to eat adequately

anosmia lack of olfaction

anosognosia inability or refusal to recognize that one has a particular disease or disorder

anoxia lack of oxygen

Antabuse trade name for disulfiram, a drug that prevents the breakdown of acetaldehyde into acetic acid, and which therefore causes people to get sick if they drink alcohol

antagonist drug that blocks the effects of a neurotransmitter, or anything that counteracts the effects of something else

antagonistic muscle muscle that moves a limb in the opposite direction from some other muscle (for example, an extensor is an antagonist of a flexor)

anterior toward the front end

anterior commissure set of axons that connects the hemispheres in the anterior part of the cerebral cortex; smaller than the corpus callosum

anterior pituitary portion of the pituitary gland, which releases growth hormone, prolactin, follicle-stimulating hormone, luteinizing hormone, adrenocorticotropic hormone, and thyroid-stimulating hormone

anterograde amnesia loss of memories for events that happened after brain damage or some other event

anthropomorphism the unjustified attribution of human characteristics to nonhuman animals

antibody Y-shaped protein that fits onto an antigen and weakens it or marks it for destruction

antidiuretic hormone (also known as vasopressin) pituitary hormone that raises blood pressure and enables the kidneys to reabsorb water and therefore to secrete highly concentrated urine

antidromic transmission propagation of an action potential toward the axon hillock from a more peripheral point on the axon; opposite of orthodromic

antigen protein on the surface of a microorganism, in response to which the immune system generates antibodies

anvil one of the small bones of the middle ear; also known as the incus

anxiolytic reducing anxiety

apex one end of the cochlea, farthest from the point where the stirrup meets the cochlea

aphagia lack of eating

aphasia lack of language abilities

apomorphine morphine derivative that stimulates dopamine receptors

apraxia inability to organize movements purposefully

arachnid any member of the spider family

arachnoid one of the membranes that cover the brain and spinal cord

ARAS *see* ascending reticular activating system

archistriatum the amygdala

arcuate fasciculus band of fibers running between Broca's area and Wernicke's area

area 17 synonym for primary visual cortex. (Other numbered areas refer to a geography of the brain described by Brodmann.)

areas V1-V5 (see **V1** through **V5**)

arecoline drug that inhibits the action of the enzyme acetyl-cholinesterase and thereby prolongs the effects of acetylcholine at its synapses

aromatic in chemistry, a chemical containing six carbon atoms with three double bonds

artificial selection change in the gene pool of a population by a breeder's selection of desired individuals for mating purposes

ascending reticular activating system system of heavily inter-connected neurons extending from the medulla into the fore-brain

aspartate an amino acid, used as a neurotransmitter

astasia inability to stand

astereognosis inability to recognize objects by touch

astigmatism blurring of vision for lines in one direction because of the nonspherical shape of the eye

astrocyte (astroglia) a relatively large, star-shaped glia cell

ataxia failure of muscular coordination

attention deficit disorder childhood condition characterized by restlessness and distractibility

atom piece of an element that cannot be divided any further

atomic number number of protons in the nucleus of an atom

atomic weight number indicating the weight of an atom relative to a weight of one for a proton

ATP adenosine triphosphate, a chemical the body uses as its main way of delivering energy where it is needed; also used as a neurotransmitter

atrophy deterioration

atropine drug that blocks the acetylcholine receptors that muscarine excites

attractivity tendency to attract sexual advances

aura distinctive sensation that occurs just before an epileptic attack

autism a condition with early childhood onset, characterized by deficit of social contact

autoceptor synonym for autoreceptor

automatism a nonreflexive yet unconscious movement

autonomic nervous system set of neurons that regulates functioning of the internal organs

autoradiography method of injecting a radioactively labeled chemical and then mapping the distribution of radiation in the brain

autoreceptor presynaptic receptor that responds to the neurotransmitter released by the presynaptic cell itself

autosomal gene gene on any of the chromosomes other than the sex chromosomes (X and Y)

AVP$_{4-9}$ metabolite of vasopressin that has been found to enhance attention toward the dominant cues in the environment

axon a single fiber that extends from a neuron

axon hillock a swelling of the soma, the point where the axon begins

8-azaguanine drug that inhibits protein synthesis

B cell type of leukocyte that matures in the bone marrow

B memory cell type of cell that immunizes the body against future attacks by a given intruder

Babinski reflex reflexive flexion of the big toe when the sole of the foot is stimulated

baclofen drug that stimulates $GABA_B$ receptors

ballistic movement motion that proceeds as a single organized unit that cannot be redirected once it begins

barbiturate class of drugs used as anticonvulsants, sedatives, and tranquilizers

baroreceptor receptor that detects the blood pressure in the largest blood vessels

basal ganglia set of subcortical forebrain structures including the caudate nucleus, putamen, and globus pallidus

basal metabolism rate of energy use while the body is at rest, used largely for maintaining a constant body temperature

base (of tympanic membrane) point at which the stirrup meets the cochlea

basilar membrane floor of the scala media, within the cochlea

behavioral medicine field that considers the influence on people's health of their eating and drinking habits, smoking, stress, exercise, and other behavioral variables

Bell-Magendie Law observation that the dorsal roots of the spinal cord carry sensory information and that the ventral roots carry motor information toward the muscles and glands

belladonna a preparation contining atropine, used to block the parasympathetic nervous system and other acetylcholine synapses

benzodiazepine class of widely used antianxiety drugs

drug that impedes transmission at the beta type of norepinephrine receptors

b-amyloid a protein found in large quantities in the plaques in brains of people with Alzheimer's disease; a possible cause of Alzheimer's disease

b-carboline type of naturally occurring chemical that binds to the same receptors as benzodiazepines

b-endorphin one type of endorphin, a neurotransmitter

beta rhythm fast, low-amplitude EEG activity

bicuculline a drug that blocks $GABA_A$ receptors

bifurcate to split into two parts

binocular vision sight based on simultaneous stimulation of two eyes

biofeedback the attempt to control internal processes by providing sensory feedback for the desired changes

biogenic amine neurotransmitter containing an amine group (NH_2), such as acetylcholine, serotonin, epinephrine, norepinephrine, and dopamine

biological clock internal mechanism for controlling rhythmic variations in a behavior

biological psychology study of the biological principles underlying behavior

biopsy removal and microscopic examination of body tissues for purpose of diagnosis

bipolar cell one of the cell types in the eye, or any other neuron with two nearly equal fibers extending from the cell body

bipolar disorder condition in which a person alternates between two poles, mania and depression

blindsight ability to point toward or look toward objects in a damaged area of the visual field

blind spot point in the retina which lacks receptors because the optic nerve exits at this point

blob cluster of neurons within the primary visual cortex, strongly responsive to the color of a visual stimulus

blood-brain barrier the mechanism that keeps many chemicals out of the brain

Borna disease viral disease that affects the nervous system of farm animals, possibly also humans, causing behavioral changes

botulin toxin chemical that blocks the release of acetylcholine

bradykinesia slower-than-normal movements

brain-derived neurotrophic factor chemical related to NGF that promotes growth of certain populations of acetylcholine-contain ing axons in the hippocampus, amygdala, cerebral cortex, and olfactory areas of the brain

brain stem the hindbrain, midbrain, and posterior central structures of the forebrain

bregma a point on the skull where the frontal and parietal bones join

bretylium tosylate a drug that facilitates the passage of sodium ions through a membrane

Broca's aphasia condition marked by loss of fluent speech and impaired use and understanding of prepositions, word endings, and other grammatical devices

Broca's area portion of the human left frontal lobe associated with speech production and comprehension of grammar

bufotenine a hallucinogenic drug

bulbar pertaining to the medulla

bulimia condition marked by episodes of overeating

butyrophenone class of neuroleptic drugs including haloperidol

^{14}**C-** labeled with the radioactive isotope of carbon

caffeine a drug that dilates blood vessels and prevents adenosine from inhibiting glutamate release

callosal pertaining to the corpus callosum

calmodulin a protein that binds calcium

calpain protein that breaks a network of molecules normally found in the dendrites

cAMP cyclic AMP

cannabinoids chemicals related to D ^{9}-THC, the component of marijuana that alters experience

Cannon-Bard theory concept that autonomic changes and emotions occur simultaneously but independently

cannula a thin tube used for delivering chemicals

capsaicin a chemical that causes neurons containing substance P to release it suddenly; the chemical responsible for the hot taste of jalapeño peppers

carbachol drug that stimulates ACh synapses

carboline type of chemical that binds to the same receptors as benzodiazepines

cardiac muscle muscle of the heart

carnivore animal that eats meat

carotid an artery of the head

castration removal of the gonads

CAT scan computerized axial tomography

cataplexy attack of muscle weakness while a person remains awake

catatonia stereotyped behavior, especially prolonged fixed positions

catecholamine compound such as dopamine, norepinephrine, and epinephrine that contains both catechol and an amine (NH_2)

cation a positively charged ion

caudal toward the rear, away from the head.

caudate nucleus one of the structures of the basal ganglia

CCK cholecystokinin

cell a unit of the body, surrounded by a membrane

cell body structure of a cell that contains the nucleus

central canal fluid-filled channel in the center of the spinal cord

central nervous system the brain and the spinal cord

central sulcus a large groove in the surface of the primate cerebral cortex, separating frontal from parietal cortex

centrifugal carrying impulses away from a given structure

centripetal carrying impulses toward a given structure

cerebellar cortex outer covering of the cerebellum

cerebellum a large, highly convoluted structure in the hindbrain

cerebral cortex layer of cells on the outer surface of the cerebral hemispheres of the forebrain

cerebrospinal fluid liquid similar to blood serum, found in the ventricles of the brain and in the central canal of the spinal cord

cerebrovascular pertaining to the blood supply of the head

cerebrovascular accident brain damage caused when a blood clot or other obstruction interrupts the flow of blood and therefore oxygen to a brain area; commonly called a *stroke*

cerveau isolé preparation in which the forebrain and part of the midbrain are separated from the rest of the midbrain, hindbrain, and spinal cord

cervical nerves the nerves leaving and entering the neck portion of the spinal cord

chlordiazepoxide one of the benzodiazepine tranquilizers (trade name: Librium)

chlorimipramine (also known as clomipramine) drug that prolongs the effects of serotonin at the synapse by inhibiting the reuptake of serotonin by the presynaptic cell

chlorpromazine drug that blocks transmission at dopamine synapses; the first antischizophrenic drug

cholecystokinin hormone released by the duodenum in response to food distention; also used as a neurotransmitter in the brain

cholinergic pertaining to the neurotransmitter acetylcholine

chorea a behavioral condition characterized by involuntary jerky movements

choreiform rapid repetitive movement resembling dance (Note that the root *chore-* is also the basis of the word *choreograph*.)

chromosome strand of DNA bearing the genes

chronic having a gradual onset and long duration

circannual rhythm repeating on a rhythm of approximately one year

circadian rhythm repeating on a rhythm of approximately one day

11-*cis*-retinal a derivative of vitamin A; when bound to an opsin, it forms a photopigment, capable of releasing energy when struck by light

classical conditioning type of conditioning produced by the pairing of two stimuli, one of which evokes an automatic response

clitoris external genital structure of a female mammal, providing sexual stimulation

clomipramine drug that prolongs the effects of serotonin at the synapse by inhibiting the reuptake of serotonin by the presynaptic cell

clonic having a spasmic alternation of rigidity and relaxation

clonidine a drug that stimulates norepinephrine presynaptic receptors (which inhibit the release of norepinephrine into the synapse)

clozapine a dibenzodiazepine drug that produces antischizophrenic effects with less risk of tardive dyskinesia than many other drugs

CNS central nervous system

cocaine strong stimulant drug that blocks the reuptake of dopamine by the presynaptic neuron

coccygeal spinal cord the most posterior segment of the spinal cord

cochlea structure in the inner ear, containing auditory receptors

coding the one-to-one correspondence between some aspect of the physical stimulus and some aspect of the nervous system's activity

cogwheel rigidity a series of jerks in a limb when it is pulled

collateral sprout newly formed branch from an uninjured axon that forms a synapse vacated when another axon was destroyed

color constancy ability to recognize the color of an object despite changes in lighting

column collection of cortical neurons, arranged perpendicular to the surface of the cortex, all of which respond to similar aspects of the stimulus

coma a state of unconsciousness from which one cannot be aroused

commissure one of the connections between the left and right halves of the brain, such as the corpus callosum or the anterior commissure

commissurotomy cutting of the corpus callosum or one of the other commissures

complex cell cell type of the visual cortex that responds best to a light stimulus of a particular shape anywhere in its receptive field; its receptive field cannot be mapped into fixed excitatory and inhibitory zones

complex partial seizure a series of minor seizures causing confusion and loss of contact with the environment for 1 to 2 minutes

compound material made up by combining elements

compulsion a forced, driven behavior

computerized axial tomography method of visualizing a living brain by injecting a dye into the blood and then passing X rays through the head and recording them by detectors on the other side

COMT catechol-o-methyltransferase, an enzyme that metabolizes catecholamines

concentration gradient difference in concentration of a solute across some distance

concordance agreement (A pair of twins is concordant for a trait if both of them have it or if neither has it.)

conditioned response (CR) response evoked by a conditioned stimulus as a result of the pairing of that stimulus with an unconditioned stimulus

conditioned stimulus (CS) stimulus that comes to evoke a particular response only after the pairing of that stimulus with an unconditioned stimulus

conditioned taste aversion avoidance of tastes that have been followed by illness

conduction aphasia difficulty in repeating what others say and in carrying on a conversation

conductive deafness hearing loss that occurs if the bones of the middle ear fail to transmit sound waves properly to the cochlea

cone one type of receptor in the retina, specialized for color vision and detailed vision

confabulation a made-up story or answer, such as one offered by an amnesic patient to fill in a gap in memory

congenital present since birth

conjugate vision movement or focus of the eyes together

consolidation formation and strengthening of long-term memories

contralateral on the opposite side of the body (left or right).

convergence (in evolution) similarity in two or more species because of similar evolutionary pressures acting on different ancestral characters

convergence (of the eyes) movement of the axes of the two eyes toward each other

cooperativity tendency for nearly simultaneous stimulation by two or more axons to produce more LTP than stimulation by just one

cornea the transparent anterior portion of the eye

coronal plane a plane that shows brain structures as they would be seen from the front

corpus callosum large set of axons that connects the two hemispheres of the cerebral cortex

cortex outer covering

cortical pertaining to the cortex

cortical spreading depression technique for temporarily inactivating one hemisphere of the cerebral cortex by applying concentrated KCl to its surface

corticospinal fluid fluid similar to blood serum, found in the ventricles of the brain and in the central canal of the spinal cord

corticospinal pathway the nerve pathway from the cerebral cortex to the spinal cord (synonym: pyramidal tract)

cortisol hormone released by the adrenal cortex that elevates blood sugar and enhances metabolism

covalent bond chemical bond between two atoms that share electrons

CR conditioned response

cranial nerve part of a set of nerves controlling sensory and motor information of the head, connecting to nuclei in the medulla, pons, midbrain, or forebrain

cretinism a type of mental retardation characterized by fairly normal appearance at birth but slow mental and physical development, caused by an iodine deficiency that leads to inadequate production of thyroid hormones early in life

Creutzfeldt-Jacob disease an inherited, usually fatal disease that leads to progressive damage to the cerebral cortex, basal ganglia, and spinal cord in middle age or old age

cribriform plate the perforated bone that separates the nasal cavity from the olfactory bulb

critical period time early in development during which some event (such as an experience or the presence of a hormone) has a long-lasting effect (synonym: sensitive period)

cross-adaptation reduced response to one stimulus because of recent exposure to some other stimulus

cross-tolerance tolerance to one drug because of exposure to a different drug

crossing over exchange of parts between two chromosomes during replication

CS conditioned stimulus

CSF corticospinal fluid

CT scan computerized axial tomography

cupula a dome- or cup-shaped structure

curare drug that blocks acetylcholine receptors on skeletal muscles

Cushing's disease condition caused by adrenal-gland tumor, often leading to emotional instability

CVA *see* cerebrovascular accident

cyclic AMP cyclic adenosine monophosphate, a chemical that serves as a second messenger within many neurons

cytoplasm fluid inside the cell membrane but outside the nucleus

D sleep synonym for REM sleep

DA dopamine

Dale's Law the statement that all branches of a neuron's axon release the same neurotransmitter

DBH dopamine-beta-hydroxylase

DBI diazepam-binding inhibitor

deafferented limb a limb in which the afferent connections have been destroyed

decerebrate lacking a cerebrum (forebrain), or having the cerebrum cut off from communication with the rest of the nervous system

declarative memory memory that a person can state, identifying it as a memory (opposite: procedural memory)

decorticate lacking a cerebral cortex

delayed alternation task task in which animals have to alternate between two responses with a delay between responses

delayed matching-to-sample task task in which an animal sees an object and then after a delay must choose the object matching the sample

delayed nonmatching-to-sample task task in which an animal sees an object and then after a delay must choose the object not matching the sample

delayed-response task assignment in which an animal must respond on the basis of a signal it remembers but which is no longer present

delusion belief that other people regard as unfounded, such as the belief that one is severely persecuted

dementia a general deterioration of intellectual functioning

dementia praecox schizophrenia

dendrite thin, widely branching fiber that emanates from a neuron

dendritic spine short outgrowth along the dendrites

denervation supersensitivity increased sensitivity by a postsynaptic cell after removal of an axon that formerly innervated it

2-deoxyglucose a chemical similar to glucose, taken up by neurons but not metabolized by them

depolarization reduction in the level of polarization across a membrane

deprenyl drug that inhibits the enzyme monoamine oxidase B; found to slow the progress of Parkinson's disease

dermatome area of skin connected to a particular spinal nerve

DES *see* diethylstilbestrol

desynchronized not occurring at the same time

desynchronized EEG a pattern of EEG recordings indicating that neurons are becoming active out of phase with one another

desynchronized sleep synonym for REM sleep

dexamethasone suppression test test of whether the drug dexamethasone suppressses the release of cortisol. (It does in most healthy normal people; it generally does not in seriously depressed people.)

dextral right-handed

DFP diisopropylfluorophosphate, a drug that inhibits the enzyme acetylcholinesterase

2-DG 2-deoxyglucose

5,7-DHT 5,7-dihydroxytryptamine

diagnosis identification of a person's disease or disorder

diazepam a benzodiazepine tranquilizer (trade name: Valium)

diazepam-binding inhibitor (DBI) brain protein that blocks the behavioral effects of diazepam and other benzodiazepines

dichotic listening task a task in which a person is presented with different messages in the two ears and is tested for which one is heard or remembered better (a test of hemispheric dominance)

diencephalon (literally, between-brain) section of the forebrain that includes the thalamus and hypothalamus

diethylstilbestrol (DES) a synthetic estrogen

differentiation formation of the axon and dendrites that gives a neuron its distinctive shape

5,7-dihydroxytryptamine a drug that destroys synaptic terminals that release serotonin

Dilantin an antiepileptic drug

diplopia perception of two images of one object

discordant dissimilar (A pair of twins is said to be discordant for a trait if one of them shows it and the other does not.)

distal located more distant from the point of origin or attachment.

distention filling up of the stomach or intestines

disulfiram a drug that binds with and inactivates enzymes that contain copper, including the enzyme that converts acetaldehyde to acetic acid and the one that converts dopamine to norepinephrine (trade name: Antabuse)

disuse supersensitivity increased sensitivity by a post-synaptic cell after a period of decreased input by incoming axons

dizocilpine a drug that blocks transmission at NMDA synapses (also known as MK-801)

dizygotic twin fraternal (nonidentical) twin

DMPEA dimethoxyphenylethylamine, a hallucinogenic drug

DNA deoxyribonucleic acid, the chemical that composes the chromosomes

dominant gene gene that exerts noticeable effects even in an individual who has only one copy of the gene per cell

domperidone a drug that blocks dopamine activity in the periphery but not in the central nervous system

dopa chemical precursor of dopamine and other catecholamines

dopamine chemical that acts as a neurotransmitter, one of the catecholamines

dopamine-beta-hydroxylase an enzyme that converts dopamine into norepinephrine

dopamine hypothesis of schizophrenia hypothesis that schizophrenia is due to excess activity at dopamine synapses

dorsal toward the back, away from the ventral (stomach) side. The top of the human brain is considered dorsal because that is its position in four-legged animals.

dorsal root ganglion set of sensory neuron somas on the dorsal side of the spinal cord

dorsolateral prefrontal cortex area of the prefrontal cortex

dorsolateral tract a path of axons in the spinal cord from the ipsilateral hemisphere of the brain, controlling movements of p eripheral muscles

dorsomedial thalamus area of the thalamus that sends axons mostly to the frontal cortex; damaged in Korsakoff's syndrome

Dostoyevskian epilepsy epilepsy that sometimes produces episodes of euphoria

double dissociation of function demonstration that one lesion impairs behavior A more than it impairs behavior B, while a second lesion impairs behavior B more than it impairs behavior A

down-regulation decrease in the amount of effect or activity at some kind of synapse

Down's syndrome condition marked by mental retardation, caused by having an extra copy of chromosome 21

drug tolerance decreased response to a drug after repeated use of it

dualist position belief that the mind exists independent of the brain and exerts some control over it

duodenum part of the small intestine adjoining the stomach

dura mater one of the membranes that cover the brain and spinal cord

dys- prefix meaning impairment

dyscalculia impairment of mathematical abilities

dyscontrol syndrome a condition marked by outbursts of unprovoked violent behavior

dysdiadochokinesia impairment of the ability to make rapid alternating movements such as clapping hands

dyslexia a specific reading difficulty in a person with adequate vision and at least average skills in academic areas other than reading

dysmnesia impairment of memory

dysphasia impairment of language

dysphoria unhappy mood (opposite of euphoria)

dyspnea impaired or labored breathing

echolocation localization of objects by hearing echos of sound waves bounced off those objects

ECS electroconvulsive shock

ECT electoconvulsive therapy

ectotherm an animal that derives its body heat mostly from the outside, therefore having a body temperature very close to that of the environment (synonym: poikilotherm)

edema excessive fluid build-up in the intercellular spaces of the body

EEG electroencephalograph

effector a muscle or gland

efferent axon a neuron that carries information away from a structure

electrical gradient difference in electrical potential across some distance

electroconvulsive therapy attempt to relieve depression or other disorders by an electrically induced convulsion

electroencephalograph device that records the electrical activity of the brain through electrodes on the scalp

electrotonic conduction conduction by the flow of electrical current

element material that cannot be broken down into other materials

emergent property position theory that the mind emerges as a new property when matter is organized in a particular way

encephale isolé a preparation in which most of the brain is separated from the spinal cord

encephalitis inflammation of the brain

encephalopathy any degenerative disease of the brain

end bulb a swelling at the end of an axon from which the neurotransmitter is released

endocrine gland organ that produces and releases hormones

endogenous self-produced, produced from within

endogenous circadian rhythm self-generated rhythm that lasts about a day

endogenous circannual rhythm self-generated rhythm that lasts about a year

endogenous depression depression that originates within the body, not as a reaction to outside events

endolymph the fluid within the labyrinth structures of the inner ear

endoplasmic reticulum a network of thin tubes within a cell that transport newly synthesized proteins to other locations

endorphin category of neurotransmitters that stimulate the same receptors as opiates

endotherm animal that generates enough internal heat to maintain a nearly constant body temperature despite changes in the environmental temperature (synonym: homeotherm)

endozepine type of naturally occurring chemical that binds to the same receptors as benzodiazepines

engram the physical representation of learning

enkephalin category of neurotransmitters that stimulate the same receptors as opiates

enuresis bed-wetting

enzyme protein that controls the rate of chemical reactions in the body

epilepsy a condition in which brain neurons have repeated episodes of excessive, synchronized activity and possibly also periods of excessive inhibition

epileptic focus the point in the brain from which an epileptic seizure originates

epileptogenic causing epileptic seizures

epinephrine chemical that acts as a neurotransmitter, one of the catecholamines

epiphenomenalism theory that the conscious mind is an accidental spin-off of brain activity

episodic dyscontrol syndrome condition marked by outbursts of unprovoked violent behavior

epithelial pertaining to the skin

EPSP excitatory postsynaptic potential, a subthreshold depolarization of the postsynaptic membrane

equipotentiality according to Karl Lashley, principle that neurons in various cortical areas contribute almost equally to complex learned behaviors

ergot a product of a fungus that sometimes grows on grains

esophagus the tube leading from the mouth to the stomach

estradiol one type of estrogen

estrogen a class of steroid hormones more abundant in females than in males for most species

estrus period when a female animal is fertile

ethology the study of the natural behavior of animals

ethyl alcohol (or ethanol) the type of alcohol that people drink (in contrast to methyl alcohol, isopropyl alcohol, and others)

etiology causation

evoked potential electrical activity recorded from the brain, usually via electrodes on the scalp, in response to sensory stimuli

evolution change in the gene pool of a population over generations

evolutionary explanation hypothesis that relates a structure or a behavior to the evolutionary history of a species

evolutionary theory of sleep concept that the function of sleep is to conserve energy at times of relative inefficiency

excitatory postsynaptic potential (EPSP) graded depolarization of a neuron

exocytosis release or extrusion of something, such as neurotransmitters, from a cell

exogenous caused by something outside the body

explicit memory memory for facts or for specific events, detectable by direct testing such as asking a person to describe a past event (opposite: implicit memory)

extensor muscle that extends a limb

extracellular outside the cells

extraocular outside the eyes

extrapyramidal disorder disruption of movement resulting from damage to part of the extrapyramidal system

extrapyramidal system movement-controlling areas other than the pyramidal system; especially the basal ganglia, red nucleus, r eticular formation, vestibular nucleus, and adjacent areas

facial nerve the seventh cranial nerve, carrying taste from the anterior two-thirds of the tongue and visceral sensations from the head; controlling facial expressions, salivation, and dilation of blood vessels in the head

Factor S small glycopeptide found in the nervous system and bloodstream of sleeping animals

fast-twitch muscle muscle that produces fast contractions but fatigues rapidly

feature detector neuron whose responses indicate the presence of a particular feature

feedback sensory information resulting from previous activities

fetal alcohol syndrome condition resulting from prenatal exposure to alcohol and marked by decreased alertness, hyperactivity, varying degrees of mental retardation, motor problems, heart defects, and facial abnormalities

fimbria band of axons along the medial surface of the hippocampus

final common path the motor neuron of the spinal cord, which participates in all types of movement

fissure a long, deep sulcus

fistula a tube into some part of the digestive system, allowing nutrients to be placed into the system or to be removed from it

fixed action pattern motor program that develops almost automatically in any normal environment

flaccid paralysis inability to move one part of the body voluntarily, accompanied by weak reflexes

flexor muscle that draws an extremity, such as an arm, toward the trunk of the body

flutamide a drug that blocks the effects of testosterone

flurazepam a long-acting benzodiazepine tranquilizer

fluvoxamine drug that inhibits the reuptake of serotonin by the presynaptic neuron

focus (in the context of epilepsy) a damaged or malfunctioning area of the brain from which an epileptic seizure originates

follicle-stimulating hormone anterior pituitary hormone that promotes the growth of follicles in the ovary

forebrain the most anterior part of the brain, including the cerebral cortex and other structures

fornix tract of axons connecting the hippocampus with the hypothalamus and other areas

Fourier analysis a mathematical method of expressing any function as the sum of a series of sine functions

fovea center of the retina, point at which receptors are most densely packed

fragile X chromosome condition in which an X chromosome has a segment that can snap off; a common cause of mental retardation in males

free nerve ending one of the somatosensory receptors

free-running rhythm circadian or circannual rhythm that is not being periodically reset by light or other cues

frequency the number of sound waves per second

frequency theory concept that pitch perception depends on differences in frequency of action potentials by auditory neurons

frontal lobe one of the lobes of the cerebral cortex

frontal lobotomy *see* prefrontal lobotomy

frontal plane a plane that shows brain structures as they would be seen from the front

FSH follicle-stimulating hormone

FTG neuron neuron of the gigantocellular tegmental field of the brain stem

functional disorder a disorder caused by experiences, not by a biological abnormality

functional explanation description of why a structure or behavior evolved as it did

fusaric acid a drug that blocks the enzyme DBH

G-protein a protein coupled to GTP; an important part of the receptor molecule found in many synapses and in certain sensory receptors

GABA gamma amino butyric acid, a neurotransmitter that generally, perhaps always, acts as an inhibitor

GABA$_A$ receptor complex structure that includes a site that binds GABA as well as sites that bind other chemicals that modify the sensitivity of the GABA site

GABAergic using GABA as a neurotransmitter

galvanic skin response measure of the electrical conductance of the skin

gamma-amino-butyric acid a neurotransmitter

ganglion (plural: **ganglia**) a cluster of neuron cell bodies, usually outside the CNS (as in the sympathetic nervous system), or any cluster of neurons in an invertebrate species

ganglion cell type of neuron within the eye

ganglioside molecule composed of combinations of carbohydrates and fats

gate theory assumption that stimulation of certain nonpain axons in the skin or in the brain can inhibit transmission of pain messages in the spinal cord

gegenhalten increased muscle tension; resistance to passive movements of the limbs

gender identity the sex with which a person identifies

gene a physical particle that determines some aspect of inheritance

general anesthetic chemical that depresses brain activity as a whole

generalized seizure an epileptic seizure that spreads quickly across neurons over a large portion of both hemispheres of the brain

generator potential local depolarization or hyperpolarization of a neuron membrane

geniculate a part of the thalamus; the lateral geniculate is important for vision, while the medial geniculate is important for hearing

genotype the total collection of an individual's genes

gigantocellular tegmental field an area of the pons with large cell bodies

Gilles de la Tourette's syndrome *see* Tourette's syndrome

glia a type of cell in the nervous system that (unlike neurons) does not conduct impulses to other cells

glioma tumorous growth of glia

globus pallidus one of the structures of the basal ganglia

glossopharyngeal nerve the ninth cranial nerve, carrying taste and other sensations from the throat and posterior one-third of the tongue; controlling swallowing, salivation, and dilation of blood vessels

glucagon pancreatic hormone that stimulates the liver to convert stored glycogen to glucose

glucose a simple sugar, the main fuel of vertebrate neurons

glutamate chemical that acts as a neurotransmitter, generally an excitatory neurotransmitter, apparently the most common neurotransmitter in the mammalian brain

glycine an amino acid used as a neurotransmitter

glycoside a compound that contains a sugar

Golgi complex a network of vesicles within a cell that prepare hormones and other products for secretion

Golgi tendon organ receptor that responds to the contraction of a muscle

gonad reproductive organ

graded potential membrane potential that varies in magnitude

grand mal seizure type of generalized seizure in which the person makes sudden, repetitive jerking movements of the head and limbs for a period of seconds or minutes and then collapses in a state of exhaustion and sleep

graphesthesia the ability to recognize figures drawn on the skin

grasp reflex reflexive grasp of an object placed firmly in the hand

gray matter areas of the nervous system with a high density of cell bodies and dendrites, with few myelinated axons

GSR galvanic skin response

GTP guanosine triphosphate, an energy-storing molecule

gyrus (plural: gyri) an outward bulge on the surface of the cerebral cortex

^{3}**H-** labeled with tritium the radioactive isotope of hydrogen

habituation decrease in response to a stimulus that is presented repeatedly and that is accompanied by no change in other stimuli

hair cell a type of sensory receptor

hair follicle receptor a receptor that responds to movements of a hair

hallucination sensory experience that does not correspond to reality

hallucinogenic drugs drugs that grossly distort perception, such as LSD

haloperidol a common neuroleptic drug

Halstead-Reitan test set of behavioral tests designed to identify the type and extent of brain damage

hair cell a type of sensory receptor shaped like a hair

hammer one of the small bones of the middle ear; also known as the malleus

Hebbian synapse synapse that increases in effectiveness because of simultaneous activity in the presynaptic and postsynaptic neurons

helper T cell type of leukocyte that stimulates added response by other immune system cells

hemi- prefix meaning half

hemianopsia blindness in the left or right visual field

hemiballismus violent motor restlessness in half of the body

hemicholinium a drug that blocks the reuptake of acetate and choline into the presynaptic cells that release acetylcholine

hemiparesis muscular weakness in half of the body

hemiplegia paralysis of the muscles on one side of the body

hemisphere either the left or the right half of the brain

hepatic pertaining to the liver

herbivore animal that eats plants

heritability a correlation coefficient, ranging from zero to 1.0, indicating the degree to which variations in some characteristic depend on variations in heredity for a given population

hermaphrodite individual whose genitals do not match the normal development for his or her genetic sex

heroin a drug that stimulates the receptors that normally respond to endorphins

Hertz cycles per second

heterozygous having two unlike genes for a given trait

hexamethonium a drug that blocks the ion pores controlled by the acetylcholine receptor without attaching to the receptor itself

5-HIAA 5-hydroxyindoleacetic acid, a serotonin metabolite

hibernation condition in which heart rate, breathing, brain activity, and metabolism greatly decrease as an adaptation to conserve energy during winter

hillock *see* axon hillock

hindbrain most posterior part of the brain, including the medulla, pons, and cerebellum

hippocampal commissure set of axons that connects the left hippocampus to the right hippocampus

hippocampal slice section of hippocampus removed from an animal and maintained in a culture medium

hippocampus large forebrain structure between the thalamus and cortex

histamine a chemical with many functions in the body, including that of neurotransmitter

histology the study of tissues

histopathology abnormalities of tissues

homeostasis tendency to maintain some variable, such as temperature, within a fixed range

homeotherm animal that maintains nearly constant body temperature over a wide range of environmental temperatures (synonym: endotherm)

homologous derived from the same ancestor

homovanillic acid a metabolite of dopamine

homozygous having two identical genes for a given characteristic

horizontal cell a cell type in the vertebrate eye, responsible for lateral inhibition

horizontal plane a plane that shows brain structures as they would be seen from above

hormone chemical secreted by a gland and conveyed by the blood to other organs whose activity it influences

horseradish peroxidase a chemical that is absorbed by axon terminals and transported to the cell body; useful as a means of anatomically tracing the origin of a given axon

5-HT 5-hydroxytryptamine, another term for serotonin

5-HTP 5-hydroxytryptophan, a precursor of serotonin

Huntington's disease an inherited disorder characterized by tremor, movement disorder, and psychological symptoms, including d epression, memory impairment, hallucinations, and delusions

HVA homovanillic acid

hydrocephalus accumulation of excessive fluid in the head

6-hydroxydopamine chemical that destroys neurons that release dopamine or norepinephrine

5-hydroxyindoleacetic acid a metabolic breakdown product of serotonin

5-hydroxytryptamine synonym for serotonin

5-hydroxytryptophan synonym for serotonin, a neurotransmitter

hypalgesia low sensitivity to pain

hyper- prefix meaning higher than normal

hypercapnia higher than normal levels of carbon dioxide in the blood

hypercomplex cell cell of the visual cortex that responds best to stimuli of a precisely limited type, anywhere in a large rec eptive field, with a strong inhibitory field at one end of its field

hyperpolarization increased electrical polarization across a membrane

hyperreflexia stronger than normal reflexes

hypertension high blood pressure

hyperthermia higher than normal body temperature

hyperventilation breathing more often or more deeply than necessary

hypnagogic hypnotic, or sleep-inducing

hypo- prefix meaning lower than normal

hypocalcemia lower than normal levels of calcium

hypoglossal nerve the twelfth cranial nerve, carrying sensation from the tongue muscles and controlling movements of the tongue

hypoglycemia lower than normal levels of glucose

hypomania condition in which people are highly energetic but not quite manic

hyponatremic having a lower than normal level of sodium

hypophysis the pituitary gland

hyposomnia lower than normal amounts of sleep

hypothalamus forebrain structure located just ventral to the thalamus

hypothermia lower than normal body temperature

hypovolemia lower than normal blood volume

hypovolemic thirst thirst provoked by low blood volume

hypsarhythmia an EEG abnormality sometimes observed in infants, characterized by random high-voltage slow waves and spikes from multiple foci

hysterectomy surgical removal of the uterus

Hz Hertz

iatrogenic caused by a physician

ibotenic acid a neurotoxin that destroys cell bodies of neurons in the area where it is applied without damaging fibers passing through

ictal pertaining to an epileptic seizure

identity position belief that the mind is the same thing as brain activity, described in different terms

ideomotor apraxia the inability to perform certain acts voluntarily, despite the ability to perform the same acts or similar ones by habit in other situations

idiopathic "self-originated," that is, of unknown cause

immune system set of structures that protects the body against viruses and bacteria

immunohistochemistry method of using the immune system to label particular types of tissues

implicit memory memory that does not require any recollection of a specific event, detectable by indirect influences on behavior (opposite: explicit memory)

impotence inability to have an erection

impulse an action potential

incomplete penetrance expression of a gene's effects to different degrees in different individuals

incus one of the small bones of the middle ear; also known as the anvil

indoleamines a set of chemicals including serotonin

infant amnesia tendency for people to recall few specific events that occurred before about age 4 or 5 years

infantile autism condition characterized by social isolation, stereotyped behaviors, abnormal responses to sensory stimuli, inappropriate emotional expressions, and abnormal development of speech and intellect

infarct an area of tissue that dies because of impaired blood supply to it

inferior below another part.

inferior colliculus part of the auditory system located in the midbrain

inferior temporal cortex portion of the cortex where neurons are highly sensitive to complex aspects of the shape of visual st imuli within very large receptive fields

inhibitory postsynaptic potential temporary hyperpolarization of a membrane

inner-ear deafness hearing loss that results from damage to the cochlea, the hair cells, or the auditory nerve

insomnia lack of sleep, leaving the person feeling poorly rested the following day

insulin hormone that increases the conversion of glucose into stored fat and facilitates the transfer of glucose across the cell membrane

interactionism theory that the mind and the brain are separate but interact with each other and influence each other

interblob area of the primary visual cortex between blobs, responsible for shape perception

intermittent explosive disorder a condition marked by outbursts of unprovoked violent behavior

interneuron a neuron that receives information from other neurons and sends it to either motor neurons or interneurons

intersex individual whose sexual development is intermediate between male and female

intraperitoneal within the abdomen, under the membrane lining of the abdominal wall

intrathecal into the space under the arachnoid membrane, one of the membranes that cover the brain and spinal cord

intrinsic neuron a neuron whose axons and dendrites are all confined within a given structure

invertebrate animal lacking a backbone

ion atom that has gained or lost one or more electrons

ionic bond chemical attraction between two ions of opposite charge

ionophore the combination of a receptor on a membrane and the channel that it controls through the membrane; an ion, such as sodium or potassium, passes through its ionophore when the channel is open

ionotropic effect synaptic effect that depends on the rapid opening of some kind of gate in the membrane

iproniazid a drug that inhibits the enzyme monoamine oxidase

ipsilateral on the same side of the body (left or right)

IPSP inhibitory postsynaptic potential

ischemia suppression of blood flow to part of the body

isocortex portions of the cerebral cortex that contain six layers

James-Lange theory notion that physiological states cause emotions, not vice versa

jet lag disruption of biological rhythms caused by travel across time zones

K-complex sharp high-amplitude negative wave followed by a smaller, slower positive wave

kainic acid chemical similar to glutamate that destroys cell bodies in contact with it but does not destroy passing axons

Kallmann's syndrome condition characterized by inability to

...nell and delayed onset of puberty

Kennard principle generalization (not always correct) that it is easier to recover from brain damage early in life than later in life

kin selection selection for a genetic trait that benefits one's relatives

kinase *see* protein kinase

kinesthesia perception of the position and motion of the muscles

kinocilium a filament found in each hair process of the hair cells of each semicircular canal; bending of the kinocilium stimulates the sensory nerve

Kleine-Levin syndrome a condition characterized by decreased activity and increased eating

Klinefelter's syndrome condition associated with an XXY chromosome pattern

Klüver-Bucy syndrome condition in which monkeys with damaged temporal lobes fail to display normal fears and anxieties

koniocortex areas of the cerebral cortex with conspicuous granular layers

Korsakoff's syndrome type of brain damage caused by thiamine deficiency, characterized by apathy, confusion, and memory impairment

Krause end bulb one type of somatosensory receptor

L-dopa chemical precursor of dopamine and other catecholamines

L-tryptophan see tryptophan

labeled-line theory concept that each receptor responds to a limited range of stimuli and has a direct line to the brain

labyrinth (1) a maze; (2) the inner ear structure that provides vestibular sensation

lactase enzyme necessary for lactose metabolism

lactate (as a noun) a breakdown produce of starches formed in the muscles during exercise

lactate (as a verb) to secrete milk

lactic acid *see* lactate

lactose the sugar in milk

lamina (plural: laminae) a layer of cell bodies separated from other cell bodies by a layer of fibers

lateral toward the side, away from the midline.

lateral fissure one of the major fissures, or folds, on the side of the cortex

lateral geniculate a nucleus of the thalamus; part of the visual system

lateral hypothalamus area of the hypothalamus in which damage impairs eating and drinking

lateral inhibition restraint of activity in one neuron by activity in a neighboring neuron

lateral interpositus nucleus a nucleus of the cerebellum critical for classical conditioning of the eyeblink response in rabbits

lateral masking difficulty reading a letter as a result of interference from adjacent letters

lateral preoptic area portion of the hypothalamus important for control of drinking

lateral ventricles two large fluid-filled cavities, one in each hemisphere of the brain

lateralization division of labor or specializations between the two hemispheres of the brain

law of specific nerve energies principle that any activity by a particular nerve always conveys the same kind of information to the brain

lazy eye a condition in which a child uses just one eye for vision, while ignoring the other eye

learned helplessness inactivity, helplessness, and possible depression resulting from a series of inescapable unpleasant experiences

lecithin a dietary precursor to acetylcholine

lenticular nucleus the putamen and globus pallidus

lesion damage to a structure

eu-enkephalin a chain of five amino acids believed to function as a neurotransmitter that inhibits pain

leukocyte white blood cell, a component of the immune system

lens structure within the eye that can focus light by increasing or decreasing its thickness

LH lateral hypothalamus or luteinizing hormone

Librium a benzodiazepine tranquilizer (chemical name: chlordiazepoxide)

lidocaine a local anesthetic that acts by blocking sodium pores in the neural membrane

ligand a chemical that binds to a receptor

ligand-gated receptor channels membrane channels that open when a ligand binds to a receptor; such channels may be either ionotropic or metabotropic

limbic system interconnected set of subcortical structures in the forebrain, including the hypothalamus, hippocampus, amygdala, olfactory bulb, septum, other small structures, and parts of the thalamus and cerebral cortex

lipids fat molecules

lithium an element whose salts are often used as a therapy for bipolar disorder

lobectomy removal of a lobe from the brain

lobotomy *see* prefrontal lobotomy

local anesthetic drugs that block action potentials in the nerves in a particular area where the drug is applied

local circuit a cluster of small neurons exchanging information over very short distances, usually with graded potentials rather than action potentials

local neuron a small neuron with no more than a short axon

locus coeruleus a small structure in the hindbrain, source of a large number of norepinephrine-containing axons

long-term memory memory for an event that was not currently in one's attention

long-term potentiation increased responsiveness to axonal input as a result of a previous period of rapidly repeated stimulation

longitudinal fissure the long groove that separates the left hemisphere of the cerebral cortex from the right hemisphere

loudness perception of the intensity of a sound

LSD lysergic acid diethylamide, a hallucinogenic chemical that blocks serotonin synapses for about 4 hours and decreases the number of serotonin receptors for days; also affects dopamine synapses

LTP long-term potentiation

lumbar puncture removal of fluid from the lumbar area of the spinal cord

Luria-Nebraska neuropsychological battery set of behavioral tests designed to identify the type and extent of brain damage

luteinizing hormone (LH) anterior pituitary hormone that stimulates the release of an ovum and prepares the uterus for implant ation of a fertilized ovum

lysosome structure within a cell that contains enzymes that break down many chemicals into their component parts

macrophage type of leukocyte that engulfs and attacks microorganisms

macropsia disturbance of vision in which objects appear larger than they really are

magnetic resonance imaging method of imaging a living brain by using a magnetic field and a radio frequency field to make atoms with odd atomic weights all rotate in the same direction and then removing those fields and measuring the energy the atoms release

magnocellular neuron large-celled neuron of the visual system that is sensitive to changing or moving stimuli

maintenance insomnia frequent awakening during the night

major depression depression of great severity and duration

malleus one of the small bones of the middle ear; also known as the hammer

mania condition of restless activity, excitement, laughter, mostly happy mood, and few inhibitions

MAM methylazoxymethanol acetate

mania a condition of uninhibited activity

manic-depressive disorder condition in which a person alternates between mania and depression; also called bipolar disorder

MAO monoamine oxidase, enzyme that converts catecholamines and serotonin into synaptically inactive forms

MAOI monoamine oxidase inhibitor

marche à petit pas a gait in which the person takes very small steps

mass action according to Karl Lashley, principle that all cortical neurons work together during learning; the more neurons, the better the performance

materialist position belief that the brain is a machine and that consciousness is irrelevant to its functioning

MBD minimal brain damage; *see* attention-deficit disorder

meatus a channel or passageway, such as the auditory meatus

medial toward the midline, away from the side.

medial forebrain bundle main ascending dopamine pathway in the vertebrate brain

medial geniculate nucleus a nucleus of the thalamus, part of the auditory system

medial superior temporal cortex an area in which neurons are sensitive to expansion, contraction, or rotation of the visual field; or to the movement of an object relative to its background

medulla hindbrain structure located just above the spinal cord

Meissner's corpuscles receptors found in hairless parts of the skin that respond to sudden movement across the skin

melatonin a hormone released by the pineal gland

membrane structure that surrounds a cell

menarche time of a woman's first menstruation

meninges the three membranes (dura, pia, and arachnoid) that cover the brain and spinal cord

meningioma a tumor that grows along the meninges

meningitis inflammation of the meninges

menopause time when middle-aged women stop menstruating

menstrual cycle periodic variation in hormones and fertility over the course of approximately one month in women

menstruation sloughing of the uterine lining about every 28-30 days in nonpregnant women

mentalism theory that the physical world exists only if a conscious mind perceives it

Merkel's disk a receptor that responds to pressure on the skin

mescaline a hallucinogenic chemical

mesencephalon (literally, middle-brain) the middle part of the brain, including the tectum, tegmentum, superior colliculus, inferior colliculus, substantia nigra, and other structures

mesolimbic system set of neurons that project from the midbrain tegmentum to the limbic system

met-enkephalin a chain of five amino acids thought to act as a neurotransmitter that inhibits pain

metabolism the chemical reactions that make energy available for use by the body

metabotropic effect effect at a synapse that produces a relatively slow but long-lasting effect through metabolic reactions

metamorphopsia a disturbance of vision in which objects appear distorted in shape

methadone a drug sometimes given to opiate addicts as a less-disabling substitute for morphine or heroin; it stimulates the receptors that normally respond to endorphins

methyazoxymethanol acetate drug that destroys neurons that are dividing or developing

methyl-para-tyrosine see alpha-methyl-para-tyrosine

methylphenidate a stimulant drug

methysergide a drug that blocks serotonin receptors

metoclopramide a drug that blocks certain dopamine receptors, producing undesirable effects on the extrapyramidal system without producing significant antischizophrenic effects

MHPG 3-methoxy-5-hydroxyphenylethylene glycol, a metabolic breakdown product of norepinephrine

mianserin an antidepressant drug that inhibits autoreceptors responsive to catecholamine neurotransmitters

microcephaly abnormal smallness of the head

microdialysis method for measuring the concentrations of chemicals in a brain area by enabling them to cross a membrane into an implanted, withdrawable tube

microelectrode a very thin electrode, generally made of glass and filled with an electrolyte solution

microglia a very small type of glia cell that removes waste material in the brain

micrographia a reduction in the size of one's handwriting

micropsia disturbance of vision in which objects appear smaller than they really are

midazolam a short-acting benzodiazepine tranquilizer

midbrain the middle part of the brain, including the tectum, tegmentum, superior colliculus, inferior colliculus, substantia nigra, and other structures

middle-ear deafness hearing loss that occurs if the bones of the middle ear fail to transmit sound waves properly to the cochlea

middle temporal cortex portion of the cortex where neurons are highly sensitive to the speed and direction of movement of visual stimuli

migration movement of neurons toward their eventual destinations in the brain

mind-body problem or **mind-brain problem** question of how the mind is related to the brain

miniature end-plate potential an EPSP in a muscle cell

minimal brain disorder or **minimal brain dysfunction** *see* attention-deficit disorder

miracle berry African berry that contains the protein miraculin

miraculin protein that alters taste buds so that acids taste sweet

mitochondrion (plural: **mitochondria**) the structure where the cell performs the metabolic activities that provide energy

mitral cell a second-order cell of the olfactory system, located in the olfactory bulb and receiving input from olfactory receptors

MK-801 a drug that blocks transmission at NMDA synapses (also known as dizocilpine)

molar in chemistry, a measure of concentration of solutions: A one-molar concentration has a number of grams equal to the molecular weight of a compound dissolved in one liter of water solution

molecule smallest possible piece of a compound

molindone an antischizophrenic drugs that acts by blocking dopamine postsynaptic receptors

monism theory that only one kind of substance exists in the universe (not separate physical and mental substances)

monoamine a class of neurotransmitters, including serotonin, dopamine, norepinephrine, and epinephrine

monoamine oxidase enzyme that converts catecholamines and serotonin into synaptically inactive forms

monoamine oxidase inhibitor drug that blocks the enzyme monoamine oxidase

monocular seeing with one eye

monozygotic twin identical twin

Moro reflex a startle reflex in infants in which the arms are thrown out as if to embrace someone

morphine a drug that stimulates the receptors that normally respond to endorphins

morphology the shape or structure of something

motion blindness impaired ability to perceive the direction or speed of movement, despite otherwise satisfactory vision

motor cortex the part of the cerebral cortex that controls movement

motor neuron a neuron that receives excitation from other neurons and conducts impulses from its soma in the spinal cord to muscle or gland cells

motor program fixed sequence of movements that occur as a single unit

MPT see alpha-methyl-para-tyrosine

MPTP 1-methyl-4-phenyl-1,2,3,6-tetrahydropyridine, a chemical which, when metabolized into MPP^+, becomes toxic to dopamine-containing cells

MPP$^+$ 1-methyl-4-phenylpyridinium, a chemical toxic to the dopamine-containing cells in the substantia nigra, capable of producing the symptoms of Parkinson's disease

MST medial superior temporal cortex, an area in which neurons are sensitive to expansion, contraction, or rotation of the visual field; or to the movement of an object relative to its background

MT the middle temporal cortex, a portion of the cortex where neurons are highly sensitive to the speed and direction of movement of visual stimuli

Müllerian duct early precursors to female reproductive structures (the oviducts, uterus, and upper vagina)

multipara a female that has given birth more than once

multiple sclerosis a disease characterized by hardening of parts of the brain or spinal cord, leading to weakness and incoordination

muricide mouse-killing

muscarine a drug that excites some acetylcholine receptors but not others

muscimol a drug that stimulates GABA receptors; can be injected in sufficient doses to suppress activity in a brain area for research purposes

muscle spindle receptor that responds to the stretch of a muscle

mutation change in a gene during reproduction

mutism failure to speak

myasthenia gravis autoimmune disease in which the body forms antibodies against the acetylcholine receptors at neuromuscular junctions

myelin sheath an insulating material that covers many vertebrate axons

myelinated axon axon covered with myelin

myelination the formation of myelin

NA noradrenalin

naloxone drug that blocks opiate receptors

narcolepsy condition characterized by unexpected periods of sleep in the middle of the day

narcosis stupor

natural killer cell type of leukocyte that destroys certain kinds of tumor cells and cells infected with viruses

natural selection increase in the frequency of certain genes because of increased reproduction by the individuals bearing those genes

Nauta method a method of applying a dark stain to degenerating axons

NE norepinephrine

negative afterimage perception resulting from the fatigue of one kind of neuron, such as the perception of green that people experience after prolonged viewing of something red

negative symptom absence of a behavior ordinarily seen in normal people

neglect *see* sensory neglect

neocortex the most recently evolved portion of the cerebral cortex

neonatal pertaining to newborns

neophobia fear of the new

neostigmine a drug that blocks acetylcholinesterase, the enzyme that breaks down acetylcholine

neostriatum the caudate nucleus and putamen

Nernst equation an equation that relates the electrical potential across a membrane to the concentrations of various ions. For example, for the sodium ion, $[Na^+]$, $E_{Na} = (RT/ZF)$ ln $([Na^+]_o/[Na^+]_i)$. In this equation, E_{Na} is the membrane potential at which Na^+ is at equilibrium; R is the gas constant, T is the Kelvin temperature, Z is the chemical valence of Na^+, F is the Faraday constant, and $[Na^+]_o$ and $[Na^+]_i$ are the concentrations of $[Na^+]$ inside and outside the membrane.

nerve a set of axons in the periphery, either from the CNS to a muscle or gland, or from a sensory organ to the CNS

nerve deafness hearing loss that results from damage to the cochlea, hair cells, or auditory nerve

nerve growth factor protein that promotes the survival and growth of axons in the sympathetic nervous system and certain axons in the brain

nerve impulse *see* action potential

nerve-muscle junction a special type of synapse from an axon onto a muscle

neural Darwinism principle that, in the development of the nervous system, synapses form somewhat randomly at first, and then a selection process keeps some and rejects others

neuritic plaque a patch that forms because of inflammation of a nerve

neuroanatomy the anatomy of the nervous system

neuroembryology the embryological development of the nervous system

neurofilament a long threadlike structure found in axons

neuroglia synonym for glia

neurohypophysis the posterior pituitary

neuroleptic drug drug that relieves schizophrenia

neurology the medical study of the nervous system

neuromodulator chemical that has properties intermediate between those of a neurotransmitter and those of a hormone

neuromuscular junction synapse where a motor neuron's axon meets a muscle fiber

neuron cell that receives information and transmits it to other cells by conducting electrochemical impulses

neuropeptide Y peptide found in the brain and digestive system; when injected into various brain locations it elicits changes in feeding, sexual behavior, body temperatue, grooming, breathing, pain, and other functions

neuropil a dense assortment of dendrites, other parts of neurons, and glia cells

neurotoxin a chemical that damages neurons

neurotransmitter chemical released at a synapse

niacin one of the vitamins

nicotine drug that, among other effects, stimulates certain acetylcholine receptors

nicotinic receptor a type of acetylcholine receptor which, in addition to being stimulated by acetylcholine, can also be stimulated by nicotine

night terror experience of intense anxiety during sleep, from which a person awakens screaming in terror

Nissl stain a method for staining cell bodies violet

NGF nerve growth factor

NMDA receptor glutamate receptor that also responds to N-methyl-D-aspartate

NMR nuclear magnetic resonance, a synonym for magnetic resonance imaging

NO nitric oxide, a chemical that acts as a neurotransmitter

nocturnal being awake at night and asleep during the day

nocturnal myoclonus a periodic involuntary movement of the legs and sometimes arms during sleep

node of Ranvier short unmyelinated section of axon between segments of myelin

non-REM sleep sleep stages other than REM sleep

noradrenaline synonym for norepinephrine

norepinephrine chemical that acts as a neurotransmitter, one of the catecholamines

normetanephrine a breakdown product of norepinephrine

nosology the classification and naming of diseases

Novocaine an anesthetic drug that acts by blocking the transport of sodium through the membrane

NPY *see* neuropeptide Y

NREM sleep *see* non-REM sleep

nuclear magnetic resonance method of imaging a living brain by using a magnetic field and a radio frequency field to make atoms with odd atomic weights all rotate in the same direction and then removing those fields and measuring the energy the atoms release

nuclei of the cerebellum clusters of neurons in the interior of the cerebellum, which send axons to motor-controlling areas outside the cerebellum

nucleus a cluster of neurons within the central nervous system, or a structure within a cell that contains the chromosomes

nucleus solitarius area in the medulla that receives input from taste receptors

nullipara a female that has never given birth

nychthemeral daily

nychthemeron one night plus one day (a 24-hour period)

nystagmus involuntary rapid eye movements

obsession a repetitive line of thinking

obsessive-compulsive disorder psychological disorder characterized by intrusive thoughts and urges to perform repetitive acts

occipital lobe one of the four lobes of the cerebral cortex

oculomotor nerve the third cranial nerve, carrying sensations from eye muscles and controlling eye movements and pupil constriction

6-OHDA abbreviation for 6-hydroxydopamine

olfaction sense of smell

olfactory bulb a forebrain structure that receives most of its input from the olfactory cells

olfactory cell neuron responsible for smell, located on the olfactory epithelium in the rear of the nasal air passages

olfactory nerve the first cranial nerve, carrying olfactory information to the brain

oligodendrocyte glia cell that surrounds and insulates certain axons in the vertebrate brain and spinal cord

omnivore animal that eats both meat and plants

onset insomnia difficulty falling asleep

ontogenetic explanation description of how a structure or a behavior develops

ontogeny development within an individual

operant conditioning type of conditioning in which reinforcement or punishment changes the future probabilities of a given behavior

opiate class of drugs that stimulate endorphin receptors in the nervous system

opponent-process theory notion that we perceive color in terms of paired opposites: white versus black, red versus green, and blue versus yellow

opsin a protein that forms one component of a photopigment

optic chiasm point at which parts of the optic nerves cross to the opposite side of the brain

optic nerve the second cranial nerve, a band of axons from the ganglion cells of the retina to the brain

optokinetic pertaining to eye movements

orbital frontal cortex an anterior area of the prefrontal cortex

orexigenic producing an increase in appetite

organ of Corti the spiral organ of the cochlea

organizing effect long-lasting effect of a hormone that is present during a critical period early in development

orientation (of a visual stimulus) the angle (such as vertical or horizontal) of a bar of light in the visual field

orthodromic transmission propagation of an action potential in the normal direction, from the axon hillock toward the end bulbs (opposite of antidromic)

orthomolecular psychiatry treatment of psychiatric problems by maintaining or establlishing optimal levels of various chemicals in the body

oscillator repetitive alternation between two movements

osmotic pressure force exerted by the concentration of a solute in water solution toward other solutions separated from it by a semipermeable membrane

osmotic thirst thirst that results from an increase in the concentration of solutes in the body

ossicle any of the three small bones found in the middle ear

otolith minute particle composed mostly of calcium carbonate, found on the surface of each otolith organ

otolith organ an organ responsible for vestibular sensation

ovary female gonad that produces eggs

OVLT organum vasculosum laminae terminalis, a brain structure on the border of the third ventricle, highly sensitive to the osmotic pressure of the blood

ovum (plural: ova) an egg

oxytocin a hormone from posterior pituitary that induces contractions of the uterus and release of milk

oxytocin hormone released by the posterior pituitary; also used as a neurotransmitter in the brain; important for sexual and parental behaviors

P300 wave positive wave occurring about 300 msec after a novel or meaningful stimulus

Pacinian corpuscle a receptor that responds to a sudden displacement of the skin or high-frequency vibration on the skin.

paleostriatum the globus pallidus

pallidum the globus pallidus

palsy paralysis

panic disorder condition characterized by occasional attacks of extreme fear, breathlessness, heart palpitations, fatigue, and dizziness

panprotopsychic identism a variant form of the identity position, according to which consciousness is present in a primitive, potential form in all matter

papaverine a chemical that inhibits the enzyme phosphodiesterase and thereby decreases the breakdown of cyclic AMP

Papez's theory of emotions the theory that emotions depend on the limbic system in the brain

papilla structure on the surface of the tongue containing taste buds

parachlorophenylalanine a drug that blocks the synthesis of serotonin

paradoxical sleep a stage of sleep characterized by complete relaxation of the large muscles but high activity in the brain; synonym for REM sleep

parallel fiber axon that runs perpendicular to the planes of the Purkinje cells in the cerebellum

parallelism (in evolution) a similarity in related species due to similar evolutionary forces

parallelism (in philosophy) the poistion that mind and brain exist separately and do not affect each other

paralysis the inability to move certain muscles

paraplegia loss of sensation and voluntary muscle control in both legs, with retention of reflexes

parastriate cortex an area of the cerebral cortex surrounding the primary visual cortex

parasympathetic ganglia the clusters of cell bodies located close to various internal organs and innervated by nerves from the cranial and sacral parts of the spinal cord

parasympathetic nervous system system of nerves innervating the internal organs, tending to conserve energy

paraventricular nucleus area of the hypothalamus which controls secretion of vasopressin; also involved in control of meal size

paresthesia abnormal or distorted sensations

parietal lobe one of the lobes of the cerebral cortex

parity the number of times a female has given birth

Parkinson's disease malady caused by damage to a dopamine pathway, resulting in slow movements, difficulty initiating movements, rigidity of the muscles, and tremors

paroxysmal pertaining to a sudden intensification of a disease or its symptoms

partial seizure epileptic seizure that begins in a focus somewhere in the brain and then spreads to nearby areas in just one hemisphere

parvocellular neuron small-celled neuron of the visual system that is sensitive to color differences and visual details

passive avoidance learning learning to suppress a behavior that is followed by punishment

paternal half-siblings people who have the same father but different mothers

pathognomonic characteristic of a disease; usefu for diagnosis

pathology the study of disease

pavor nocturnus night terrors

PCPA parachlorophenylalanine, a drug that blocks the synthesis of serotonin

PEA phenylethylamine, a hallucinogenic chemical that occurs naturally in the body

penetrance the degree of expression of a gene

peptide chemical compound composed of two or more amino acids

peptide hormone hormone composed of a chain of amino acids

peptide neurotransmitter a neurotransmitter composed of a chain of amino acids

periaqueductal gray area of the brain stem that is rich in enkephalin synapses

perikaryon the cell body of a neuron

perinatal around the time of birth

periodic movement in sleep repeated involuntary movement of the legs and sometimes arms during sleep

peripheral nervous system nerves outside the brain and spinal cord

permeability the ability of an ion to cross a membrane

perseveration tendency to repeat a previously learned response even though some other response is currently more appropriate

PET scan positron-emission tomography, a method of mapping activity in a living brain by recording the emission of radioactivity from injected chemicals

petit mal seizure type of generalized seizure in which the person stares, unresponsive to the environment, for a period of seconds, making no sudden movements, except perhaps for eye-blinking or a drooping of the head

peyote a hallucinogenic chemical derived from mushrooms

PGO wave pattern of high-amplitude electrical potentials that occurs first in the pons, then in the lateral geniculate, and finally in the occipital cortex

phantom limb a sensation that feels like a body part even after that part has been amputated

pharmacological dose a dose of a hormone or other substance that exceeds the normal range that occurs in nature (Compare: physiological dose.)

phenothiazine a class of neuroleptic drugs including chlorpromazine

phenylalanine an amino acid

phenylketonuria inherited inability to metabolize phenylalanine, leading to mental retardation unless the afflicted person stays on a strict low-phenylalanine diet throughout childhood

phenylpyruvate a breakdown product of phenylalanine

pheromone odorous chemical released by one animal that affects the behavior of other members of the same species

phosphodiesterase a drug that breaks down cyclic AMP

phospholipid a compound including phosphorus and fatty acids; phospholipids form the lipid bilayer of a cell membrane.

phosphorylation attachment of a phosphate group (PO_4) to a protein or other compound

photopigment chemical in the rods and cones that releases energy when struck by light

phrenology nineteenth-century theory that personality types are related to bumps on the skull

phylogeny the evolutionary origin of a species and its genetic relationship to other species

physiological dose a dose of a hormone or other substance that stays within the normal range that occurs in nature (Compare: pharmacological dose.)

physiological explanation concept that relates an activity to how the brain and other organs of the body function

physiology mechanisms of control of body functions

physostigmine a drug that antagonizes the enzyme acetylcholinesterase

pia mater one of the membranes that surround the brain and spinal cord

pica the eating of nonfood substances, such as dirt

picrotoxin a drug that blocks GABA synapses

carpine a drug that excites acetylcholine receptors

erection erection of the hairs ("gooseflesh" in humans)

eal gland a hormone-releasing gland inside the brain

ch the experience that corresponds to the frequency of a
und

pituitary gland endocrine gland attached to the hypothalamus; its secretions regulate the activity of many other hormonal glands

PKU phenylketonuria

place theory concept that pitch perception depends on which part of the inner ear has cells with the greatest activity level

placebo an inactive substance given as a substitute for an active drug, usually as a treatment for a control group in an experiment

Planaria a flatworm

planum temporale area of the temporal cortex that is larger in the left than in the right hemisphere for most people

plaque structure formed from degenerating axons and dendrites in the brains of people with Alzheimer's disease

PMS premenstrual syndrome

pneumoencephalography x-ray photography of the head after injecting air into the fluid spaces of the head

PNS parasympathetic nervous system or peripheral nervous system

POA the preoptic area

poikilotherm animal that maintains the body at approximately the same temperature as the surrounding environment (synonym: endotherm)

polarization an electrical gradient across a membrane

poliomyelitis paralysis caused by a virus that damages cell bodies of the motor neurons

polygenic controlled by many genes

polypeptide YY peptide found in the brain and digestive system; when injected into the paraventricular nucleus of the hypothalamus, it increases feeding

polysomnograph a combination of EEG and eye-movement

records, and sometimes other data, for a sleeping person

pons hindbrain structure, anterior or ventral to the medulla

positive symptom presence of a behavior not seen in normal people

positron-emission tomography a method of mapping activity in a living brain by recording the emission of radioactivity from in jected chemicals

postcentral gyrus gyrus of the cerebral cortex just posterior to the central gyrus; a primary projection site for touch and ot her body sensations

posterior toward the rear end

posterior parietal cortex part of the parietal lobe of the cerebral cortex; important for attention to a visual object

posterior pituitary portion of the pituitary gland

postictal following an epileptic seizure

postmortem after death

postpartum after giving birth

postrolandic the postcentral gyrus (primary somatosensory cortex)

postsynaptic membrane a specialized area of the membrane of a postsynaptic cell that is responsvie to the neurotransmitter

postsynaptic neuron neuron on the receiving end of a synapse

posttraumatic stress disorder condition characterized by periodic outbursts of anxiety, panic, or depression provoked by remin ders of a traumatic experience

posture position of body parts with respect to one another and to gravity

precentral gyrus gyrus of the cerebral cortex just anterior to the central sulcus; a primary point of origin for axons of the pyramidal system of motor control

prefrontal cortex the most anterior portion of the frontal lobe of the cerebral cortex

prefrontal lobotomy surgical disconnection of the prefrontal cortex from the rest of the brain

premenstrual syndrome tension and discomfort reported by certain women during the day or days just before menstruation

premorbid a person's condition prior to the onset of a disease

premotor cortex area of the frontal cortex, just anterior to the primary motor cortex, active during the planning of a movement

prenatal before birth

preoptic area brain area adjacent to the anterior hypothalamus, important for temperature control

prestriate cortex *see* parastriate cortex

presymptomatic test exam to predict the onset of a disease, conducted before any symptoms appear

presynaptic inhibition an effect on a presynaptic neuron that decreases its tendency to release its transmitter

presynaptic neuron neuron on the releasing end of a synapse

presynaptic receptor receptor located on the terminal at the tip of an axon

presynaptic terminal the tip of an axon, the point from which the axon releases chemicals

primary motor cortex area of the frontal cortex just anterior to the central sulcus; a primary point of origin for axons of the pyramidal system of motor control

primary visual cortex area of the cortex responsible for the first stage of visual processing

primate member of the mammalian order including humans, monkeys, apes, and their relatives

priming phenomenon that seeing or hearing a word or words increases the probability that a person will soon use those same words

priming stimulus a stimulus that increases the response to a later stimulus

primipara a female that has given birth once

proband the individual who is the starting point for an investigation, especially a study of the relatives of a disordered individual

procedural memory memory of how to do something (opposite: declarative memory)

proceptivity tendency to approach a partner and actively seek sexual contact

Procion brown or **Procion yellow** a fluorescent stain that is injected into a neuron through a glass electrode that was used to record from the cell; used to mark the cell for later identification

progesterone hormone that prepares the uterus for the implantation of a fertilized ovum

prognosis prediction of the outcome of a disease

progressive disorder a disorder that grows progressively more severe

projection an extension of axons from one area to another

prolactin a hormone released by the anterior pituitary that stimulates lactation in mammary glands

proliferation the production of new cells

projection a set of axons from one brain structure to another. If axons extend from structure A to structure B, we say that the fibers "project" from A onto B.

propagation of the action potential transmission of an action potential down an axon

prophylactic preventing disease

proprioceptor receptor that is sensitive to the position and movement of a part of the body

prosencephalon (literally, forward-brain) the forebrain, which includes the diencephalon (thalamus and hypothalamus) and the telencephalon (cerebral cortex, hippocampus, basal ganglia, and other subcortical structures)

prosopagnosia inability to recognize faces

prostaglandin E_1 chemical produced during an infection, which stimulates an increase in body temperature

protein molecule composed of a long string of amino acids

protein hormone protein released as a hormone

protein kinase enzyme that transfers a terminal phosphate group (PO_4) group from ATP onto a protein

proximal located close (approximate) to the point of origin or attachment.

pseudobulbar similar to the conditions resulting from damage to the medulla

pseudohermaphrodite individual whose sexual development is intermediate between male and female

psilocin a hallucinogenic chemical

psychomotor seizure a minor seizure causing confusion and loss of contact with the environment for 1 to 2 minutes

psychophysical observation report by human observers concerning their perceptions of various stimuli

psychosomatic illness illness for which personality or experience influences onset or recovery

psychosurgery brain surgery conducted to change behavior

puberty onset of sexual maturity

pulvinar a nucleus of the thalamus

punishment event that decreases the future probability of the preceding response

pupil opening in the eyeball through which light enters

Purkinje cell a neuron type in the cerebellum; the type of neuron responsible for all the output from the cerebellar cortex to the cerebellar nuclei

pursuit eye movement eye movement that follows a moving target

putamen one of the structures of the basal ganglia

pyramid swelling in the medulla where pyramidal system axons cross from one side of the brain to the opposite side of the spinal cord

pyramidal neuron neuron with a cell body shaped like a pyramid, generally having a long axon

pyramidal system structure originating mostly in the precentral and postcentral gyri whose axons cross in the pyramids of the medulla and extend to neurons in the medulla or spinal cord; important for control of discrete movements

PYY *see* polypeptide YY

quadriplegia loss of sensation and muscle control in all four extremities, due to a cut through the spinal cord above the level controlling the arms

quantum the minimum size of an EPSP or IPSP in a postsynaptic neuron

quazepam a long-acting benzodiazepine tranquilizer

quiet biting attack swift, calm attack with few signs of emotional arousal

quiet sleep synonym for non-REM sleep

quinolinic acid chemical resembling glutamate that kills certain neurons by overstimulating them

rabies disease caused by a virus that attacks much of the brain, especially the temporal lobe

racemic a mixture of the D- and L- forms of a stereochemical

radial glia a type of glia cells that guides the migration of neurons and the growth of their axons and dendrites during embryological development

radial maze apparatus with many arms radiating from a central point, generally with food at the end of some or all of the arms

raphe system group of neurons in the pons and medulla whose axons extend throughout much of the forebrain; a system contributing to the control of sleep

rapid eye movement (REM) sleep sleep stage with rapid eye movements, high brain activity, and relaxation of the large muscles

rCBF regional cerebral blood flow

reactive depression depression that arises as a reaction to experiences

reactive disorders disorders that originate as reactions to experiences

reception the absorption of physical energy by a receptor

receptive field region of the receptive surface (such as retina or skin) that can excite or inhibit a given neuron

receptivity tendency to respond favorably to sexual advances

receptor a neuron specialized to be highly sensitive to a specific type of stimulation

recessive a gene that exerts noticeable effects only in an individual who has two copies of the gene per cell

recombination a reassortment of genes during reproduction, sometimes leading to a characteristic that is not apparent in either parent

red nucleus nucleus midbrain structure whose axons join the dorsolateral tract of the spinal cord, controlling distal muscles of the body such as those in the hands and feet

reference memory memory for general principles

reflex automatic response to a stimulus

reflex arc circuit of neurons and their connections that is responsible for producing a reflex

refractory period brief period following an action potential, when the cell resists reexcitation

regional cerebral blood flow method of estimating activity of different areas of the brain by dissolving radioactive xenon in the blood and measuring radioactivity from different brain areas

reinforcement event that increases the future probability of the preceding response

relative refractory period time after an action potential, when a stimulus must exceed the usual threshold to produce an actio n potential

releasing hormone hormone that the hypothalamus releases and that flows through the blood to the anterior pituitary

REM behavior disorder condition in which people move around vigorously during REM sleep

REM sleep sleep stage with rapid eye movements, high brain activity, and relaxation of the large muscles

remission relief from the symptoms of a disease

renin a hormone released by the kidney that leads to constriction of the blood vessels

repair and restoration theory of sleep concept that the function of sleep is to enable the body to repair itself after the exertions of the day

resection removal of a large portion of a structure in the body

reserpine a drug that causes depletion of norepinephrine, dopamine, and serotonin from their vesicles

resting potential electrical potential across a membrane when a neuron is at rest

reticular formation network of neurons in the medulla and higher brain areas, important for behavioral arousal

retina rear surface of the eye, lined with visual receptors

retinal *see* 11-*cis*- retinal

retinal disparity difference in locations of the two retinas stimulated by a single item

retinex theory concept that the cerebral cortex compares the wavelengths of light coming from different parts of the retina at a given time and from that comparison determines a perception of color for each object

retinoblastoma a tumor of the glia cells in the retina

retinotopic arranged in such a way that each anatomical subdivision of a brain area corresponds to sensation from a different part of the retina

retrograde amnesia loss of memory for events that occurred before brain damage

retrovirus virus made of RNA that makes a DNA copy of itself

reuptake reabsorption of a neurotransmitter by the presynaptic terminal

rhinencephalon a traditional term for certain structures of the forebrain that were once believed to be all active in olfactory perception; nearly synonymous with the limbic system

rhombencephalon (literally, parallelogram-brain) the hindbrain, consisting of the medulla, pons, and cerebellum

ribosome the site at which the cell synthesizes new protein molecules

Ritalin trade name for methylphenidate, a stimulant drug sometimes used as a treamtent for attention deficit disorder

RNA ribonucleic acid, a chemical whose structure is determined by DNA and that in turn determines the structure of proteins

rod one type of receptor in the retina, specialized for vision in dim light

Rolandic fissure a deep groove in the cerebral cortex, also known as the central sulcus, which divides the frontal lobe from the parietal lobe

rooting reflex reflexive head turning and sucking after a touch on the cheek

rostral toward the head (or toward the front of the head, where the nostrils are)

Ruffini ending a receptor that responds to stretch of the skin

saccade rapid movement of the eyes from one fixation point to another

saccadic eye movement sudden shift of the eyes from one target to another

saccule a large subdivision of the membranous labyrinth of the vestibular system; one of the otolith organs

SAD *see* seasonal affective disorder

sagittal plane a plane that shows brain structures as they would be seen from the side.

salicylate or **salicylic acid** aspirin

saltatory conduction alternation between action potentials at nodes and a more rapid conduction by the flow of ions between nodes

satiety a feeling of fullness after a meal

sc (in the context of injections) subcutaneous (under the skin)

scala media the middle chamber in the cochlea, also known as the cochlear duct

scala tympani the lowermost chamber in the cochlea

scala vestibuli the uppermost chamber in the cochlea

schizophrenia disorder characterized by deteriorating ability to function in everyday life and some combination of hallucinations, delusions, thought disorder, movement disorder, and inappropriate emotional expressions

Schwann cell glia cell that surrounds and insulates certain axons in the periphery of the vertebrate body

scintillating scotomata areas of the retina in which one sees only sparks

sclerosing hardening

SCN *see* suprachiasmatic nucleus

scopolamine drug that inhibits muscarinic acetylcholine synaptic transmission by competing with acetylcholine for receptor sites

scotoma (plural: scotomata) a gap in the visual field, in which a person cannot see anything

scratch reflex reflexive alternation of extension and flexion of a limb in response to irritation of the skin

season-of-birth effect tendency for people born in winter to have a greater probability of developing schizophrenia than do people born in other seasons

seasonal affective disorder (SAD) period of depression that reoccurs each winter

second messenger chemical activated by a neurotransmitter, which in turn initiates processes that carry messages to several ar eas within the neuron

secondary visual cortex area of the visual cortex responsible for second stage of visual processing

sedative something that reduces activity and excitement

selective permeability tendency to permit certain chemicals but not others to cross a membrane

self-stimulation of the brain response reinforced by direct electrical stimulation of a brain area

semicircular canal canal lined with hair cells and oriented in three planes, sensitive to the direction of tilt of the head

semipermeable membrane a membrane that permits only water and a few other molecules to cross

sensitive period a time (generally early in life) when a particular type of experience has an especially strong and long-lasting effect on the development of behavior (synonym: critical period)

sensitization increase in response to mild stimuli as a result of previous exposure to more intense stimuli

sensory extinction tendency to respond first and more strongly to stimuli on the same side of the body as brain damage, as opposed to stimuli on the opposite side

sensory neglect ignoring of stimuli on the side of the body opposite an area of brain damage

sensory neuron a neuron specialized to be highly sensitive to a specific type of stimulation

sensory store extremely brief storage of sensory information

septum a limbic system structure located anterior and medial to the hippocampus

serial-lesion effect tendency for recovery to be more complete after a series of small lesions than it is after a single, large lesion

serotonin chemical that acts as a neurotransmitter, one of the monoamines

serotonin reuptake blocker drug that blocks reuptake of serotonin by the presynaptic neuron that released it

serum the liquid portion of the blood, free of cells

servomechanism a mechanism that produces behaviors that are influenced by feedback from previous behaviors

set point level at which homeostatic processes maintain some variable

sex-limited gene gene that exerts its effects primarily in one sex because of activation by androgens or estrogens, even though members of both sexes have the gene

sex-linked gene gene on either the X or the Y chromosome

sex role the set of activities and dispositions presumed to be common for one sex in a particular society

sham feeding preparation in which everything an animal swallows leaks out a tube connected to the esophagus or stomach

sham lesion control procedure for an experiment, in which an investigator inserts an electrode into a brain but does not pass a current

sham rage motor components of attack that are not directed against any target

shape constancy ability to perceive the shape of an object despite the movement or rotation of the object

short-term memory memory for an event that just happened

simple cell type of visual cortex cell that can be excited by a point of light anywhere in the excitatory part of its receptive field and inhibited by light anywhere in the inhibitory part

simultanagnosia inability to detect more than one object at a time or to shift attention from one stimulus to another

sine-wave grating an alternation of light and dark over space following a sine wave function

sinistral left-handed

skeletal muscle muscle that controls movement of the body with respect to the environment (such as arm and leg muscles)

sleep apnea inability to breathe while sleeping

sleep spindle burst of 12 to 14 Hz brain waves lasting at least half a second

slow-twitch muscle muscle that produces less vigorous contractions without fatiguing

slow-wave sleep (SWS) stages 3 and 4 of sleep that are occupied largely by slow, large-amplitude brain waves

smooth muscle muscle that controls movements of internal organs

sodium-potassium pump mechanism that actively transports sodium ions out of the cell while simultaneously drawing potassium io ns in

soma structure of a cell that contains the nucleus

somatic nervous system nerves that convey messages from the sense organs to the CNS and from the CNS to muscles and glands

somatosensory cortex the portion of the cerebral cortex that responds to touch and other body information

somatosensory system sensory network that monitors the surface of the body and its movements

somatotopic arranged in such a way that each anatomical subdivision of a brain area corresponds to sensation from a different part of the body

somesthetic somatosensory

somnambulism sleep-walking

somnolence sleepiness, drowsiness

spasm sudden, violent, unpleasant involuntary contraction of muscles

spasticity increased tension of muscles and increased resistance to stretching of them

spastic paralysis lack of voluntary movements in part of the body due to interruption of fibers from the brain to the spinal cord

spatial summation the summation of effects of activity from two or more synapses onto a single neuron

specific anosmia inability to smell a particular chemical

specific hunger an increased preference for foods containing a specified vitamin, mineral, or other nutrient

sphenoidal pertaining to the sphenoid bone at the base of the skull

spike an action potential

spinal cord portion of the central nervous system found within the spinal column

spinal nerve nerve that conveys information between the spinal cord and either sensory receptors or muscles in the periphery

spindle *see* muscle spindle

spiral ganglion ganglion that receives its input from the cochlear nerve of the ear

spiroperidol a drug that binds to dopamine receptors

splanchnic nerve nerve from the thoracic and lumbar parts of the spinal cord and the ganglia of the sympathetic nervous system to the digestive organs

splanchnic nerves nerves carrying impulses from the thoracic and lumbar parts of the spinal cord to the digestive organs and from the digestive organs to the spinal cord

splenium posterior part of the corpus callosum

spontaneous firing rate speed of action potentials that a neuron produces in the absence of synaptic input

sprouting the branching of axons to fill synaptic spaces left vacant by the loss of other axons

stapes one of the small bones of the middle ear; also known as the stirrup

startle response the response one makes after a sudden, unexpected loud noise or similar sudden stimulus

state-dependent memory memory that is better recalled under the same physiological conditions that were present during learning

statoacoustic nerve the eighth cranial nerve, carrying auditory and equilibrium information to the brain

statoconia synonym for otolith organs

status epilepticus a series of repeaated epileptic convulsions not separated by periods of normal consciousness

stereocilia stiff portions of the hair cells in the semicircular canals of the inner ear

stereognosis recognition of objects by the sense of touch

stereoscopic depth perception ability to detect depth by comparing the slightly different inputs from the two eyes

stereotaxic atlas an atlas of the location of brain areas relative to external landmarks

stereotaxic instrument device for the precise placement of electrodes in the head

steroid hormone hormone that contains four carbon rings

stimulant drugs drugs that tend to increase activity and arousal, at least in most people under most circumstances

stirrup one of the small bones of the middle ear; also known as the stapes

strabismus condition of the two eyes pointing in different directions

stretch reflex reflexive contraction of a muscle in response to a stretch of that muscle

striate cortex area of the occipital cortex with distinctly striped appearance; synonymous with primary visual cortex, or V1

striated muscle muscle that controls movement of the body with respect to the environment (such as arm and leg movements)

striatum the caudate nucleus and putamen

stroke brain damage caused when a blood clot or other obstruction interrupts the flow of blood and therefore oxygen to a brain area

strychnine drug that antagonizes synaptic activity of glycine

stupor unconsciousness or unresponsiveness

subacute between acute and chronic

subarachnoid space area beneath the arachnoid membrane that surrounds the nervous system

subcutaneous under the skin

subdural beneath the dura; a membrane that surrounds the nervous system

subfornical organ brain structure adjoining the third ventricle of the brain, where its cells monitor blood volume and relay information to the preoptic area of the hypothalamus

subplate cell temporary neuron that forms just below the area where the cerebral cortex is developing

substance P a neurotransmitter released by nerves sensitive to pain

substantia nigra midbrain area that gives rise to a path of dopamine-containing axons to the caudate nucleus and putamen

subthalamic nucleus one of the structures of the basal ganglia

sulcus (plural: **sulci**) a fold or groove that separates one gyrus from another

sulpiride drug that binds certain dopamine receptors; sometimes used as a treatment of schizophrenia

summation *see* spatial summation, temporal summation

superior above another part.

superior colliculus midbrain structure active in vision, visuomotor coordination, and other processes

superior olive a nucleus in the medulla, shaped somewhat like an olive, that receives input from both ears

superior temporal cortex a part of the temporal lobe of the cerebral cortex important for visual perception of the movement of an object

supplementary motor cortex area of the frontal cortex active during the planning of a movement

suprachiasmatic nucleus area of the hypothalamus where damage disrupts the biological clock

supraoptic nucleus an area of the hypothalamus which controls secretion of vasopressin

SWS slow-wave sleep

Sydenham's chorea a condition producing rapid, jerky, involuntary movements

Sylvian fissure one of the major fissures, or folds, on the side of the cortex

sympathetic nervous system network of nerves innervating the internal organs that prepare the body for vigorous activity

symptomatic resulting from a disease

synapse point of communication between two neurons or between a neuron and a muscle

synaptic block cessation of firing of a postsynaptic cell due to an excess of neurotransmitter at a synapse

synaptic cleft the space separating presynaptic from postsynaptic cell

synaptotagmin a protein embedded in neuronal membranes, probably responsible for opening and closing the channel that admits calcium ions to the cell

synchronized happening at the same time

synchronized sleep sleep with a high prevalence of slow, large-amplitude EEG waves

syncope fainting; a sudden temporary loss of consciousness

syndrome a set of symptoms that regularly occur together

synergistic effect tendency for two influences acting simultaneously to produce more than twice the effect of either influence acting alone

synesthesia a sensation of one type induced by stimulation of another type (for example, a hearing sensation stimulated by light)

synkinesia an unintentional movement accompanying a voluntary movement

T cell immune system cells which directly attack intruder cells or stimulate added response by other immune system cells

tabes dorsalis paralysis caused by a virus that damages cell bodies of motor neurons

tachycardia excessively rapid heartbeat

tangle collection of disrupted axons and dendrites found in the brains of people with Alzheimer's disease

tardive dyskinesia side effect of neuroleptic drugs characterized by tremors and other involuntary movements

taste bud structure on the tongue that contains taste receptors

tectorial membrane a flexible membrane that extends along the length of the cochlea

tectum roof of the midbrain in mammals; the main visual area of fish, amphibians, reptiles, and birds

tegmentum dorsal part of the midbrain

telencephalon (literally, end-brain) section of the forebrain that includes the cerebral cortex, hippocampus, basal ganglia, and other subcortical structures

template model which one tries to copy

temporal lobe one of the lobes of the cerebral cortex

temporal summation combination of effects of more than one synaptic input at different times

terminal button a swelling at the end of an axon from which neurotransmitter is released

termination insomnia tendency to awaken early and to be unable to get back to sleep

testicular feminization condition in which a person lacks the mechanism that enables androgens to bind to genes in a cell's nucleus

testis male gonad that produces testosterone and sperm

testosterone one type of androgen

thalamotomy removal of part of the thalamus

thalamus structure in the center of the forebrain

theophylline a stimulant; acts by antagonizing the ability of phosphodiesterase to inactivate cyclic AMP

thermoneutral zone the range of environmental temperatures for which an individual can maintain a normal body temperature without expending much effort (e.g., neither shivering nor sweating)

theta wave irregular, jagged, low-voltage brain wave at a rhythm of 4 to 7 cycles per second

thiamine (vitamin B_1) a chemical necessary for the metabolism of glucose

thioridazine a phenothiazine derivative that produces antischizophrenic effects with less risk of tardive dyskinesia than many other drugs

Thorazine trade name for chlorpromazine, a drug commonly used in the treatment of schizophrenia and related conditions

thought disorder impaired thinking, such as difficulty understanding and using abstract concepts

threshold level of depolarization at which a brief stimulation triggers a rapid, massive electrical change by the membrane

thyroid hormone hormone produced by the thyroid gland

thyrotropin releasing hormone a hormone from the hypothalamus that causes the pituitary to release TSH, a hormone that stimulates the thyroid gland

tonic characterized by continuous tension

tonic immobility posture in which an animal becomes limp and motionless except for an occasional muscle twitch

tonotopic arranged in such a way that each anatomical subdivision of a brain area corresponds to a different auditory tone

Tourette's syndrome a behavioral condition characterized by tics and other repetitive movements

tract a set of axons within the CNS

tranquilizer drug that decreases anxiety

transcutaneous electrical nerve stimulation method of relieving pain by applying prolonged, mild electrical shock to the arms, legs, or back

transduction the conversion of physical energy by a receptor into an electrochemical pattern in the neurons

transmitter *see* neurotransmitter

transverse plane a plane that shows brain structures as they would be seen from above

traveling wave wave which travels along a surface, producing some displacement at all points, though possibly more at some than at others

tremor involuntary trembling

TRH thyrotropin releasing hormone

triazolam a short-acting benzodiazepine tranquilizer

trichromatic theory theory that we perceive color by means of the relative rates of response by three kinds of cones, with each kind maximally sensitive to a different set of wavelengths

tricyclic drug that prevents the presynaptic neuron from reabsorbing catecholamine or serotonin molecules after releasing them

trigeminal nerve the fifth cranial nerve, carrying sensations from the skin of the face, and controlling chewing and swallowing movements

trisomy 21 having three strands of chromosome 21 per cell, leading to Down's syndrome

trochlear nerve the fourth cranial nerve, carrying sensations from eye muscles and controlling eye movements

trophic factor chemical that promotes survival and activity

tryptophan amino acid, a precursor in the synthesis of serotonin

TSH a hormone from the anterior pituitary gland that stimulates the thyroid gland

tubero-infundibular pathway a neural pathway connecting two parts of the hypothalamus, the medial preoptic area and the median eminence

Turner's syndrome genetic condition of anatomical females with an XO chromosome pattern

turnover release and resynthesis of a neurotransmitter

tympanic membrane the eardrum

tyrosine an amino acid that serves as the precursor to several neurotransmitters

UCR unconditioned response

UCS unconditioned stimulus

ulcer open sore on the lining of the stomach or intestines

unconditioned response response automatically evoked by an unconditioned stimulus

unconditioned stimulus stimulus that automatically evokes an unconditioned response

unipolar disorder mood disorder with only one extreme (or pole), generally depression

unit a neuron or part of a neuron, from which electrical potentials can be recorded

unmyelinated lacking a myelin sheath

up-regulation increase in the amount of effect or activity at some kind of synapse

UR unconditioned response

US unconditioned stimulus

utricle a large subdivision of the membranous labyrinth of the vestibular system; one of the otolith organs

V1 primary visual cortex, area responsible for the first stage of visual processing

V2 secondary visual cortex, area responsible for the second stage of visual processing

V3 area of the visual cortex responsible for detailed spatial perception, especially in and near the fovea

V4 area of the visual cortex responsible for processing color information

V5 area of the visual cortex responsible for motion detection (synonymous with area MT)

vacuole a small space or cavity

vagus nerve the tenth cranial nerve, carrying taste from the epiglottis, pharynx, and larynx, and sensations from the neck, throax, and abdomen; controlling swallowing, and parasympathetic nerves to the heart and viscera

Valium a benzodiazepine tranquilizer (chemical name: diazepam)

vascular pertaining to the blood vessels

vasopressin (also known as antidiuretic hormone) posterior pituitary hormone that raises blood pressure and enables the kidneys to reabsorb water and therefore to secrete highly concentrated urine

ventral toward the stomach, away from the dorsal (back) side. (*Venter* is the Latin word for belly. It also shows up in the word *ventriloquist*, literally meaning *stomach-talker*.)

ventricle any of the four fluid-filled cavities in the brain

ventromedial hypothalamus one of the nuclei of the hypothalamus, in which damage leads to faster stomach emptying and in creased secretion of insulin

ventromedial tract a path of axons in the spinal cord providing bilateral control of the trunk muscles

vertebrate an animal species with a spinal cord

vertigo a hallucination of moving or being moved

vesicle tiny, nearly spherical packet near the axon terminals filled with the neurotransmitter

vestibular nucleus cluster of neurons in the brain stem, primarily responsible for motor responses to vestibular sensation

vestibular organ component in the inner ear that detects tilt of the head

vestibular sensation the sense of orientation of the head with respect to gravity

visual agnosia impaired ability to identify visual objects, despite otherwise satisfactory vision

visual cortex the part of the cerebral cortex that receives the most direct input from the visual system

visual field the part of the world visible to the eyes at a particular moment

VMH ventromedial hypothalamus

volley principle tenet that a sound wave of a moderately high pitch may produce a volley of impulses by various fibers even if no individual fiber can produce impulses in synchrony with the sound waves

voltage-activated gate gate in the neuronal membrane that opens as the membrane becomes depolarized

W cell type of ganglion cell that is only weakly responsive to visual stimuli

Weigert stain a stain that is absorbed by axon terminals and transported to the cell body; useful as a means of finding the cell bodies that gave rise to a given axon

Wernicke's aphasia condition marked by poor language comprehension and great difficulty remembering the names of objects

Wernicke's area portion of the human left temporal lobe associated with language comprehension and naming

white matter area of the nervous system consisting mostly of myelinated axons

Williams syndrome type of mental retardation in which the person has good use of language in spite of extremely limited abilities in other regards

Wilson's disease a progressive degeneration of the basal ganglia of the brain

Wisconsin card-sorting task task in which a person first sorts cards according to one rule and then reshuffles them and sorts them according to a different rule

Wolffian duct early precursors to male reproductive structures

word blindness loss of the ability to read, despite otherwise adequate vision

word deafness an inability to understand spoken language despite the abilities to read, to speak, and to hear

working memory memory for current but temporary information

X cell small ganglion cell, located mostly in or near the fovea

X chromosome a chromosome of which female mammals have two and males have one

XO chromosome pattern condition of anatomical females having only one sex chromosome, an X, per cell; also known as Turner's syndrome

XXY chromosome pattern condition of anatomical males with an extra X chromosome, also known as Klinefelter's syndrome

XYY chromosome pattern condition of anatomical males with an extra Y chromosome

Y cell relatively large ganglion cell, distributed fairly evenly throughout the retina

Y chromosome a chromosome of which female mammals have none and males one

yohimbine a drug that antagonizes a_2 adrenergic receptors, which are presynaptic receptors that inhibit the release of norepinephrine from the presynapatic cell

Young-Helmholtz theory proposal that we perceive color by means of the relative rates of response by three kinds of cones, with each kind maximally sensitive to a different set of wavelengths

zeitgeber (German for "time-giver") stimulus that resets a biological clock